Provided as an educational service by Marketing Velocity - Specialist in Contractor Marketing Systems

**www.AffluentContractor.com**

Warning: Don't Spend One Hard Earned Penny On Marketing Until You Read This Guide!

# "The Home Improvement Contractors Guide To Marketing & Sales"

## THE SECRET STRATEGIES FOR EXPLOSIVE LEAD GENERATION REVEALED

- How to avoid 5 marketing rip offs.
- 14 Costly misconceptions about marketing.
- What marketing method works best right now for contractors.
- 4 Mistakes to avoid when choosing a marketing company.
- Why you want a trackable no staff marketing system.
- The consequence (and difference) of value and price.
- 4 Steps to a profitable marketing system
- The "One Second" In House Marketing Analysis

DAVID HAWKE

Dear Home Improvement Contractor,

Choosing a marketing message, campaign or system isn't easy.

Why? Because you're bombarded with misleading information, confusing claims and simply bad information from super low prices and high pressure sales tactics to unqualified marketers and their worthless methods.

How do you ever find a qualified competent method to market your business and make you money?

You start by reading this contractors guide.

**In this fact filled booklet you'll discover:**

- How to avoid choosing the wrong marketing methods.
- 14 Costly misconceptions about marketing.
- What marketing methods work best right now for contractors.
- 4 Mistakes to avoid when choosing a marketing company.
- The importance (and difference) of value and price.
- Why you want a strong healthy trackable no staff marketing system.
- 100% No Risk Guarantee.
- 4 Steps to your own profitable trackable no staff marketing system.

We wrote this guide to help you better understand marketing and sales.

Now with this information you can make an informed, intelligent decision and if you have any questions about marketing or sales in your business, you're invited to call us at 423-443-4329.

We've dedicated our business to educating contractors. We'll be happy to help you in every way.
Sincerely,

*David Hawke*

David Hawke
Marketing Velocity - Specialist in Contractor Marketing System

# Contents

How To Avoid Five Marketing Ripoffs 7

14 Costly Misconceptions about Contractor Marketing 15

What Marketing Method Works Best For Contractors Right Now? 29

4 Mistakes To Avoid When Choosing A Marketing Company 36

Why You Want A Trackable No Staff Marketing System 41

The Consequence (and difference) Of Value And Price 45

100% No Risk Guarantee 47

Four Steps To A Profitable Marketing System 48

The "One Second" In House Marketing Analysis 49

Wrap Up 54

"Special FREE Bonus Offer Worth $497.00" 55

# The Home Improvement Contractors Guide To Marketing & Sales

## How To Avoid Five Marketing Ripoffs

**Number 1** is running a marketing campaign when you have a bad or no business reputation for potential customers to see. With the Internet today, anybody can immediately go do a search for your business and find out if your customers have been happy or unhappy with you – or if you have no reputation, maybe they think your customers are just indifferent to you. Having a good reputation online is critical and getting that built before you start marketing with other campaigns should be done, especially if you have a bad reputation.

This is true no matter what kind of marketing campaign you are thinking about running - if it's television, radio, newspaper, direct mail, valpak – it doesn't matter. Studies show one of the first thing people do when they see your ad is go to the Internet and do a search on your business, there they'll see what other people have to say about you and your business.

If you have people leaving bad reviews online about your business it's extremely important to at least respond to those bad reviews and get them cleared up as 70% of people who read online reviews reported taking those as serious as a personal recommendation from a friend.

The way you can capitalize on this is to get your customers to go to your businesses Google+ page (do a search for "your company name" + "city you operate in") and write a review on your business. Obviously, you want to do this with the customers that who have had a good experience with your business. Get them write a review about the experience they've had with your business. Now anyone who searches your business online will see your happy customers experience which will give them the reason they're looking for to call you instead of your competition.

I will talk later in this book about exactly how and when to ask customers to place these reviews.

**Number 2** is "too good to be true" pricing. Nothing comes without a cost. I'm sure you've bid against contractors who low balled their bid just to get the job. Too good to be true pricing is the same in marketing as it is in contracting. When you're competing with a contractor and you know their price is too low, you know that person is leaving something out of the bid and after they contract the job they're jack their price up at the end and get that customer to pay more money than was originally asked for. They're purposefully misleading the customer just to get the job. In marketing, it's the same thing. The difference is, at the end, the price probably won't get jacked up, but you're also not going to get the benefit that should have been produced if the marketing had been done correctly. So, too good to be true pricing is the same in any field. If your gut tells you it's too good to be true, don't go with the low-ball bidder for your marketing, period.

**Number 3** when a marketing salesperson tells you, "We'll create the ad for you." I fell into this one when I was contracting. I payed a local radio station for an ad and I didn't really know what to say in the commercial. So I relied on the salesperson to make the ad for me. To make a long story short, I spent a lot of money and got zero sales from it. A very expensive lesson! Marketing salespeople are great at selling marketing. Typically they are not great at creating marketing messages. You need a marketing message that generates leads no matter if you're using radio, television, print, direct mail or any other form of advertising – wherever you decide to spend your money, make sure you have a message that is going to resonate with your prospects and generate leads and sales for you. And, if at all possible you should use an ad that has been used by others and previously proven to work, there are a lot of examples of this being done with great success in direct response marketing. After all, the goal of advertising is to make profit, right?

**Number 4** you have to create your businesses brand to be successful. This is an absolute, one hundred percent lie, although the salespeople who tell you this are just repeating what they've been told by the industry, they aren't lying to you on purpose.

First of all branding is expensive and because it's based on number of impressions and people recalling those impressions when they decide to do business, it's impossible to track.

That's good for the companies who sell branding campaigns, because branding campaigns actually make very few sales for small and medium businesses, but you'll lack proof. If you call to complain about not receiving enough sales to even pay for the campaign, you'll be told branding takes time and you need to invest in another six months worth of ads to really get the full benefit.

It's common practice for even large companies to fire and hire marketing firms about once a year because of non-performing ad campaigns. It usually takes six months, eight months, or even a year, before companies realize their branding campaign isn't working. Most will then fire their existing marketing firm and move on to another. The problem is, the majority of companies on this hamster wheel are either uninformed or uneducated about marketing and tend to go back to the same type of non-trackable branding campaign and unfortunately for them, start the process all over again. Another six, eight or twelve months and still nothing's happening, by now the company feels like it's hemorrhaging money and STILL NO SALES are coming in. You can see how this type of marketing can easily cost the unknowing businesses the ultimate price of having to lay off employees, go into bankruptcy and possibly even close their doors for good leaving a trail of destruction that effects the business, it's employees, vendors and customers.

The goal for your marketing is to generate a profit - PERIOD. If you don't agree please stop reading this book right now, your marketing will always suffer. If you're looking for a better way, a way to make as much money as you'd like and have maximum control, keep reading.

If you send out a direct mail ad, place an ad on the radio or buy a TV spot and it doesn't generate any activity in your business, then there's either a problem with the message or the prospect you've sent the message to. Now you have to study that piece of marketing and determine what made the ad fail. In numerous cases of advertising, it's simply the piece of advertising doesn't ask people to do anything. There has to be a call to action (branding campaigns rarely have this). That call to action tells people to go to a website to get more information or make the phone call to schedule a job. To increase success you should have a call to action in every piece of marketing you do. If you don't have a call to action in your marketing, you are wasting money. Make prospects offers and tell them what they need to do to take advantage of your offer, it's really not that difficult.

**Number 5** you have to have a website to compete in business today. This one I'm a little leery of because I agree you definitely should have a website to compete in business and there are numerous reasons why. But it's also a ripoff when people come and tell you have to have a website, they'll also say, nobody is looking in the Yellow Pages and nobody is reading the newspaper anymore. That's an absolute lie. There are people looking in the Yellow Pages and there are people looking in the newspaper. People are looking in every marketing medium available. The question is, does your desired clientele read the paper or use the yellow pages? If you're advertising in the newspaper, your clientele probably needs to be above fifty years old and somewhat affluent because those are the large majority of people who still read the paper. The thing that doesn't work is bad ads in the newspaper, most ads as we just talked about have no call to action and are not set up to get a response from the prospect.

But this portion is about websites right? Let's get back on track. I will tell you a website that has been designed to generate leads and get found when prospects are searching for you, will definitely help your business. There are people searching online for contractors to do business with every day. In fact as of the time of writing this book there are 33,100 people per month searching Google for siding contractors in the United States.

So what should a prospect see when they visit your website? The basic information you should have listed on your website is: why a prospect should choose you over your competitor, make prospects who visit your website an offer to do business with you or at the very least to leave you their contact information so you can continue to market to them, list your contact information, and have customer testimonials that can be easily read.

Also, your website will work for you twenty-four/seven, will never take a vacation and does not go on sick leave. This makes having a quality lead generation style website a strongly suggested sales and marketing tool.

One of the most valuable aspects of your website is your ability to easily track your marketing methods. If you run a val-pak or a direct mail campaign for instance and you drive those people to your website to give them more information, to download a book, or just to leave their contact information so you can go back and make contact with them again, you are able to see exactly what is happening with your ad and if it is a success or not.

> **Most purchases are made after 4-8 contacts with you. Getting their information and staying in touch with them puts you in control.**

If someone visits your website and does not leave their information before they leave your site, you have no way of knowing who they were and they become a wasted lead.

# The Home Improvement Contractors Guide To Marketing & Sales

**Websites let you tell the prospect as much as they need to know for no extra cost...**

If you're going to send a direct mail campaign and you choose to send a postcard, there's only so much information you can physically print on the postcard itself. Instead if you tell people a little bit of information, what I call teaser copy, you can direct them to your website for more information and greatly enhance your chance of getting a lead or making a sale with that same postcard. You can also put an unlimited amount of information on the website and it costs nothing extra.

If you're not using your website like this, I'd suggest you start. Your website should be a tool to not only generate leads and get you new customers but also track your marketing efforts and save you money on advertising that is not generating a profit!

Remember, your website needs a call to action to be effective. The nice thing about websites is you can create a different web page (this is referred to as a landing page) for each active marketing campaign you have. So if you are running a direct mail campaign, a radio campaign, a TV campaign and have a Yellow Pages ad, all those can be directed to a single website, but they can go to different web pages so everything is tracked and you will know with absolute certainty what's working best.

Now you have the ability to know if a customer came from the TV, radio, direct mail or wherever else you're advertising. You find out which marketing piece is actually sending you back dollars as profit. Keep those campaigns running shut down the one's not generating profits and grow your business while spending less. Especially in a tough economy, you need to stop wasting your money on advertising that doesn't work or at the very least go back and evaluate your ads to figure out why they didn't work. Is it not reaching the right prospects or is it just a bad message to the prospect? This gives you insight into what your marketing dollars are doing for your business. Putting you in control rather than just hoping and praying your marketing dollars bring you back a return.

I'm sure you'd agree, hoping and praying really doesn't generate profits. On the other hand knowing what your marketing dollars are doing gives you complete control and allows you grow your company at the pace you decide.

# 14 Costly Misconceptions about Contractor Marketing

**1. Your campaign must run for six to 12 months to be successful.**

This is absolute BS. It does not have to run for six to 12 months to work. Your campaign should work straight out of the gate. If it does not, there's a problem and it needs to be looked at immediately.

A lot of brand marketing companies want to sell you large packages of marketing. When it doesn't work for the first month or two and you call and ask why it is not working maybe even ask to cancel the contract, they will tell you, "People have to see your ad around ten times or so before they are willing to buy from you."

This makes no sense whatsoever. Why would somebody need to see an ad ten times as opposed to doing business with you the first time? I promise nobody is sitting there rocking in their easy chair thinking, "Well, I have another nine times, and when I see that ad nine more times, I will do business with this company." It just doesn't work like that.

Your campaigns do not have to run for six to 12 months in order for them to be effective.

**2. Your marketing budget should be 10% of your gross sales.**

Why would you put a cap on your marketing budget? If I give you a marketing campaign and tell you, "Spend $1,000 on this and you will get $2,000 back," would you do it? If it works, how many times would you do it? You would probably do it as many times as you possibly could. Why would you not spend $10,000 on that campaign and get $20,000 back, or even spend $100,000 and get $200,000 back? It just makes sense.

When a marketing campaign is working, you do it as much as you can to make as much money as you can. It's that plain and simple. The only real reason to budget your marketing is if it isn't working and is draining your company of capital. And, in the case where it's not working, there's really no reason to spend anymore money on the campaign at all, is there? In the last chapter we talked about tracking your marketing - now set up some tracking for your marketing so you can stop wasting money on campaigns that are not working and allocate those dollars to methods that generate leads and grow profits.

**3. The only reason to market is to get new customers.**

The majority, likely as high as 98% of businesses operate with this thought but it is absolutely untrue.

If you are willing to try it, you'll find one of your most valuable, profit producing marketing campaigns will be to existing customers. Of course I assume as existing customers these people already know, like, and trust you. They've done business with you and they are predisposed to do business with you again without for much selling, this can be as easy as sending them an offer for a new product.

Marketing to existing customers is not only more profitable, it is easier and it costs less to run these campaigns because you do not have to persuade the customer you are better than your competitors, they already know it.

Did you know 68% of customers do NOT do business with a company again simply because of indifference? They just don't feel appreciated and are not communicated with on a regular basis. If your customers do not hear from you at least on a monthly basis you need to put together a system to fix this problem, I can assure you it is costing you money.

A simple newsletter sent monthly can raise the lifetime value of a customer exponentially, increasing your profit per customer by thousands or possibly even hundreds of thousands of dollars.

### 4. Marketing to the largest crowd possible is a good idea.

It is a good idea if you are looking to go broke. "Everybody" should not be on your radar as part of your target market. You may read this and be thinking, "I am a contractor. I work on houses. Everybody who has a house is my customer or could be my customer or should be my customer."

This is not true. There are many houses in which people's income ranges will not match up with being able to pay you for your services as well as many other reasons which will remove people from your target market. It is often said, "Marketing to everybody is marketing to nobody" if you will narrow your target market and speak directly to that market in your marketing your leads generated will increase and you'll be much more successful.

When I was running my contracting company, my best customers were upper middle-class married couples in their upper 50's. They were easy to work with, had money and were happy to pay me. I was also able to gear my marketing messages specifically toward them and their wants. It made for a good relationship and made me a lot of money.

Who is your best market? If you can figure that our and market directly to them even though it is not the largest crowd you could market to, it will make you much more effective. You will make more sales; you will spend less money on your marketing; and, obviously, have more profit in your business by condensing your market and pinpointing the people who are truly going to be good customers for you.

Targeting like this allows you to eliminate problem customers as well. Now you're choosing who you'll do business with and what type of projects you'll do for them, giving you the ultimate control. If,like a lot of other contractors, you're doing projects you'd rather not do just because you were able to close the job, changing things up and choosing a target market can mean the difference in enjoying the business and hating it.

Isn't it time you started enjoying the time you're at work?

**5. You have to participate in social media.**

Again, this is absolutely not true. Social media seems to be the hottest trend and if you haven't joined in the conversation everyone is likely telling you, you should. While it is important to be aware of social media and what may or may not be said about your business. To say you have to participate in social media is absolutely wrong.

It also is not something you want to jump into without having a plan. If you intend to use social media to market your business, be sure you have a plan with set goals and a clear idea of what types of information you'll be posting. Have a scheduled time each week or maybe even a few times a week to add something to your social media channels (Facebook, Linkedin, Twitter and YouTube are a few of the most popular channels) to get information out to the people who have liked, followed, Tweeted, shared or whatever other term they'll come up with in the future.

If you are going to start a social media campaign, make sure you have a social media plan and determine your goals. There are a couple of things you need to create a successful social media plan.

You need to know how often you are going to put content out and on which channel, what the content is going to be about, and to whom you are talking. This takes us back to the last segment which is targeting the crowd or person who is perfect for your business. Last but not least you need to create a goal for your social media, a goal will allow you to determine when your social media campaign is a success.

We've found with no plan most businesses who decide to start marketing with social media will be abandon or use it very inconsistently. If you're looking to generate leads from your social media efforts make sure you have a plan.

## 6. Marketing is about your business.

Again, this is absolutely wrong. Marketing is not about your business. Marketing is about your customer and what your customers want and need.

Your marketing should focus on your customers' needs, but it should also try to sell them on what they want. People do not always buy what they need, but they will buy what they want.

Target it towards wants and fulfill with peoples needs; and always tell your customer what benefits they'll get by doing business with you. Most contractors as well as other companies for that matter want to tell their prospects how long they've been in business, have cheesy one liners like: You deserve the best. Don't tell them they deserve the best, tell them what the best is and then how to get it. Which is of course by doing business with you.

## 7. The first step in marketing is creating an ad and blasting it to everyone who can use your services.

We already kind of covered this one. I just want to reiterate how important it is to have a targeted prospect and build your ads around them.

I see this all the time. People want to blast their ad to the whole city. Sometimes they blast it to their entire state! It's just a great way to try to go broke by marketing to people who really are not qualified prospects. Ok, enough on that.

## 8. Your Web site is an online brochure.

Most people use their Website as an online brochure. You read the same kind of information on their Website that you would find on their business card. Maybe a bit more of an expanded view of it. Sometimes there are blogs. Sometimes there are pictures and those do help.

Your Website, should be much more than an online brochure. Web sites are capable of doing lots of things and becoming very valuable business tools. As we've already talked about one of the most important jobs a web site should be capable of is the tracking of marketing campaigns. You can send people to various pages on your Web site from marketing campaigns you are running. By doing so, you are able to track the traffic or track the customers clicking on each page and have a clear view of what leads and sales your marketing is generating for you.

You now know exactly how many people responded to an ad or at least how many people had an interest. From there you can track further and see how many people took advantage of an offer in a particular ad. It is a great way to target your marketing and make sure marketing dollars spent are generating more dollars coming in than are going out.

You can also target phone calls. I know many times you want customers to make a phone call to the business or to listen to a recorded message. With today's technology it easy to gat a tracking phone number set up. You can have a different phone number in each and every advertising campaign you run. These tracking numbers will tell you exactly how many people made a call due to a specific piece of advertising as well as how long the call lasted. What's more if you choose, you can even monitor the calls to see what is being said. This works great when you want to find out what your best salespeople are saying to get the sale!

## 9. We had to cut marketing to save money.

This has to be the most ridiculous statement I have ever heard from any business. The only reason to cut your spending on marketing is that it is not making money or you just want the business to whiter like and unwatered flower in the desert.

If you have to cut marketing because of reduced sales or not enough sales coming in, then your existing marketing is obviously not working. Now is the time you need to get a good marketing system that has been proven to work and will generate a return on your investment dollars and implement the system.

Pretty much, the only reason you would save money by cutting a marketing budget is because you do not have enough sales in the first place. Marketing done right generates sales and is an investment not a cost. When you are not getting enough sales, you need to increase your marketing not decrease it.

Obviously you need to invest in quality marketing. This doesn't mean to throw money at radio just because the radio salesperson came to see you last week. You need to put your money into marketing campaigns you will be able to track. You should know exactly what is going on with a campaign and know your money is working for you and not being wasted. Tracking is the only way to do that, if you can't track it, don't do it.

## 10. Marketing is expensive.

There are all kinds of marketing ads you see in the Super Bowl each year that cost $1 million or $2 million. Marketing obviously can be very expensive.

However, if you are using marketing campaigns designed to get a response from somebody, and you are tracking those campaigns to make sure they are working, marketing is not expensive. Instead, the investment it makes you money. If you have a limited budget you may only choose to print and mail 100 letters this week. It will not cost much and when you generate some sales from one you can increase the amount you spend next week. Before you know it you'll be sending thousands of letters each month and will be building an extremely valuable business asset.

Whether you plan to work the rest of your life at the business you build or you'd rather build a thriving business and sell it for millions and retire. This is a great way to do it.

No matter what the amount, if you spend $1 million per week on your advertising and it brings in $2 million per week, it was not expensive. It made you $1 million. Marketing should not be expensive; it should be a profitable investment.

## 11. The Yellow Pages are dead.

With the Yellow Pages, you will hear many people, especially those trying to sell you a Website or a search engine optimization tool, tell you the Yellow Pages are dead and nobody uses them anymore.

To an extent, they are right. Much of the younger crowd Googles things nowadays. The Smart Phones have come into play and there are a lot of them out there with people using them to find the products and services they want. It's important to understand this. Whether it's finding a contractor or the best piece of pizza in town, they are using the internet.

However, Yellow Pages do still work. There are people who run Yellow Pages ads and they are getting a good response from those ads. Do not rule out Yellow Pages just because somebody tells you it doesn't work anymore.

If you are putting a good ad in there, designed to get a response from somebody like we talked about earlier in the book, your ad should be making you money. If you put a good ad in there which you know works and it does not make you money, it does not necessarily mean the Yellow Pages don't work. It means the Yellow Pages do not work for your market.

Maybe the people who are your best customers are not looking at the Yellow Pages. This is something you need to figure out. However, do not assume any marketing avenue is dead just because it is old or because everybody now uses the Internet.

Most Yellow Pages ads don't work because they suck! Just today I looked at contractor ads in the Roofing, HVAC, Siding, Sunrooms and Swimming Pool sections. The headline on each ad was the business name. Remember we talked about this earlier. Marketing is not about you it's about the customer. Your business name or slogans like "We Treat You Right" "You Deserve The Best" "We Specialize" "147 years experience" will not get you noticed or a sale. It has to be about a benefit the customer will get from doing business with you. By the way all of those are actual slogans I read in the Yellow pages... Except for the 147 years experience. It always amazes me how people think years of service will get them more jobs. This is contracting not the post office, time in service does not count. Giving the customer what they want and building trust is the only thing that counts here.

A lot of people do use the Internet to market their businesses, but these other marketing methods are working like gangbusters in many instances. I will tell you a secret. Direct mail is one of the largest drivers of sales out there, bar none. Whether it is radio, TV, Internet ads or Websites, direct mail converts more people to sales than any other method at this point in time.

**12. You must brand your business.**

We kind of talked about branding earlier. Branding, I think, is a misunderstood word. When people think about branding, most people think about the design, the logo, the look of the business name or the colors for the business.

Those things are able to be branded and you want people to see your business the same way each time. You do not want to have a green truck and a purple building and entirely mismatch. At the same time, branding is not nearly as important as actually getting somebody to pick up the phone and call you to make a purchase or get you to come talk to them about a job.

Direct response advertising is designed to get people to contact you and at least let you know they are interested in your product. You can look at this as having prospects raise their hands to let you know they are a prospect worth going after. You can brand for years and years and never get a sale out of it or you can send a direct marketing piece which will generate sales immediately. It's your choice.

Meanwhile, if your trying to brand your business you are spending all of this money without generating any sales. You can potentially market your business right out of business. Brand marketing just does not work as well for small and medium businesses as well as direct response. And, even when there is moderate success the same dollar amount given a direct response focus will generate more leads and result in higher profits.

**13. Marketing big is best.**

We've already decided you want to consolidate your target market for maximum effectiveness.

But this time by marketing big I mean marketing in 15 different places. Maybe you are running TV ads and radio ads and magazine ads and running ads on the Internet. You want to be a lot of places in order for your message to be seen by the people who are your best customers.

Do it in moderation, though and make sure each media is generating a profit. Many times if you do not have a large amount of money to put into marketing, choosing to dominate just a small number advertising spaces will prove to be very profitable.

For example you can direct your radio ad to a webpage that triggers a direct mail campaign. In turn this leads to a phone call asking your company to come look at a job.

Make sure a marketing campaign is working by tracking each piece. Once you figure out what works best, you can start growing it from there. You can branch out and put your message on the radio, on the TV, mail larger geographic areas and participate in some of the more costly methods out there.

We recommend starting off kind of small to make sure things are working. Do some testing in the beginning. Once you have a marketing campaign that's proven itself to make sales and generate profit, then start expanding.

**14. When you have an email list, you should add everybody you find or come in contact with to your email list.**

This one is one of my pet peeves. It does two things. First - it puts a bunch of people on your email list who are not targeted customers. Second - it makes people mad.

Just because you get somebody's business card, their name and their email address does not mean you should put them on an email list and begin emailing them.

You should be courteous and ask people. If you think a person is a good, qualified prospect for you, you should ask them if they would like to receive your email newsletter or whatever you are sending by email. It might be coupons, a newsletter or a combination.

However, do not just load everybody onto an email list just because you wound up seeing their name and their email address. It does not work. It makes people mad and will actually cause people to go to your competitor and do business with them in some cases.

There you have the "14 Costly Misconceptions about Contractor Marketing." Check through this list. Are you doing any of these things or have you done them in the past?

Make sure when the next sales person comes in to sell you advertising, they do not put you into one of these traps causing you to spend money without being able to track the ad response through tracking either with your website or a tracking telephone number.

## What Marketing Method Works Best For Contractors Right Now?

I'm going to make a blanket statement that any kind of marketing media (TV, Radio, Newspaper, Yellow Pages, Direct mail, online ads, social media etc...) works. If it wasn't working people wouldn't be using it. So now that we know it all works , the important part is to determine whether or not your current marketing media, is the best way to get your message in front of your target client. For instance, if your target prospect is 70 year old men and you're using Facebook ads advertise, you will not be very happy with the results. However if your target prospect is 25-45 year old professional people, you'd very likely have a good result.

So you see it isn't a matter of if the marketing media works it's a question of if your target prospect is likely to see your ad there.

If you're using a marketing media and it's not working, you've got to assess whether it's a problem with the message you're sending to your prospect or a problem with the media which is essentially putting your message in front of the wrong people.

So either you're prospect targeting is not right or maybe the message to market isn't right. But I want to be clear all of the marketing media's do work when targeted correctly.

I'm going to talk about three of the top marketing media platforms which should be working great for contractors right now. So, if you're using these methods and your marketing is not working, again, you have to assess who the prospect is that's receiving the message and if the message is really built to get that specific prospect to take action and contact you.

**1. Direct Mail** - You may have heard direct mail just doesn't work anymore, because of all the new methods available like online marketing and social media. Here's the deal, the people telling you this are either trying to sell you on spending your ad dollars with them or they just don't know what they're talking about!

Direct mail accounts for the majority of sales made by most industries today. In fact, I know personally, some of the big companies who use infomercials to sell are doing direct mail campaigns that out perform their infomercial in a big way. Also, everyone seems to think sending an email is better these days than an old fashioned letter. Using direct mail will make you stand out from your competition and give you an advantage. I'm willing to bet you'll be the only contractor making offers to prospects this way. Which is an advantage all by itself

> **70% of people** renewed a relationship with a business because of it's direct mail
> **94% of people** took action on promotional offers sent to them via direct mail
> **40% of people** tried a new business after receiving it's direct mail

There are many neighborhoods in the United States a contractor could target for new customers and quite literally retire there. To do this you simply dominate the neighborhood.

You make sure everyone in the neighborhood gets your marketing message and offers. Choosing a neighborhood or two or three and focusing your marketing right there will cause people looking to have a project done on their home to come to you when they're ready to get started or least to get a quote. And, if you've been marketing correctly, you'll have built a relationship (you can use properly laid out newsletters to easily do this) with them so now, they know you, like you and trust you as the expert they need to do business with instead your competitor. (*Hint* You can also charge higher prices and still make the sale using this method).

2. **Keeping in touch with your existing customers** is the highest ROI you'll get when you're marketing. These people already know, like and trust you. You can keep in touch with them pretty inexpensively just by sending a monthly newsletter. The newsletter can be sent through snail mail (post office) or through email. It doesn't really matter how you choose to do it, just keeping in touch with them and providing them with quality information about their neighborhood and homes as well as telling them what's new in your business will keep them coming back. Be sure to make your newsletter interesting. Don't give them a lot of technical jargon and be sure the reader will get a benefit and enjoy reading it. It's a great way to get repeat business and also if laid out right, to get referrals and new prospects coming through to your business.

**3. Places for Business**, you probably know it, as Google + or Google Places. In August 2012 Google places converted every business listing they had over to a Google+ page. This method is truly one of the most important places you can showcase your business today.

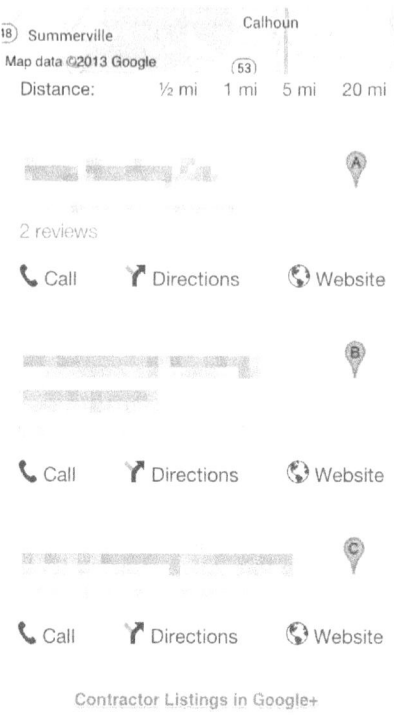

Contractor Listings in Google+

Many people are searching for the products and services they want, online. According to Google, 165,000 people in the United States searched the phrase "Home Improvement Remodeling" in one month alone. The thing that stands out and makes the search term unique is, there is no City name attached to the search phrase. Using Google+ will allow you to get your business found when a prospect is searching for products and services but not using location specific search terms. In other words how do the search engines know if the person searching wants a contractor in Chattanooga Tennessee or Seattle Washington? The answer is Google+, the search engines know the geographic location of the person doing the search and will automatically make the assumption the person would like a contractor near their location. When the search is done like this, local companies Google+ pages will show up in the search results.

If you'd like, you can see how this works for yourself. Go to Google.com and enter a search for "Home Improvement Remodeling" (do not use the quotes). Even though you did not enter your physical location you can see local companies showing up in your search results, right? Is your company listed in those results? If not, a qualified search engine optimization (SEO) company can help you get listed. Be careful, not all SEO companies are created equal. That's a subject for another book, but just in case you'd like to know more on how to get your company's listing to the first page on the search listings give us a call or send us an email, we'll be glad to explain how you can achieve better rankings.

You may be saying "Hey! Google isn't the only search engine on the internet, what about Yahoo and Bing?" That's absolutely true and Yahoo and Bing both have the same type of Local Business listings and your business should be listed with them as well. The reason we're only talking about Google is because 67% of people using the internet to search products and services use Google.

Aside from getting your business seen by more prospects, a listing in the Google+ business directory also makes it incredibly easy to call you with just the click of one button. People can also get directions to your office or visit your website as seen in the diagram on the previous page. You'll also notice people can give reviews on your business there. The first listing in the diagram shows a business with 2 reviews, (business names have been removed for privacy). Studies have shown 72% of prospects take these online reviews as serious as a recommendation from a close personal friend. Which makes getting your clients to review you online a profitable activity for any business.

I promised you earlier in the book I'd tell you how and when to get your clients to review your business, so here you go: When should you ask your customers to write a review on your business? Right after you've completed a project for them and they are happy. This is the moment when they are the happiest they are ever going to be with you in regard to this project and the most likely to write a review for you. Also, if you want to increase the odds of them actually writing this review, provide them with a card that has the web address with the location of your Google+ page and maybe a QR code they can scan with a smart phone so it is as easy for them to write as possible. Even when you make it easy not everyone will review you, don't get your feelings hurt. People are busy. It's still very much worth your time to get as many of your customers as possible to tell the rest of the world, how great it is to do business with you and what it is they liked about doing business with you.

So those are the marketing methods working best right now for contractors. I urge you, go out and at least try one of these. Start getting some new clients, sell again to existing clients and build your business. Remember, make sure you're tracking every ad you run.

Something else you need to be aware of here is Google, Yahoo and Bing all created these local pages for your business without you even asking. Anyone can review your business online whether or not you choose to claim your businesses listing or not.

Do you know if your business has one of these page listings? It's easy to check and see if your business already has a local business page which has been set up for you. Do this by going to Google and do a search for "Your Business Name" + "Your City" it should look like this "my contracting business chattanooga".

How important is this for your business? We just dramatically increased a customers business by helping them get some reviews and get their Google+ page found in the search listings. It took the number of times people saw their business online from an average of 4-6 times per day up to an average of 100 times per day. You decide.

## 4 Mistakes To Avoid When Choosing A Marketing Company

You've probably been contacted, approached, written to and probably even hounded by a marketing salesperson in the past. This booklet certainly isn't about running down salespeople, when you boil everything down every one of us is a salesperson. You sell your contracting and home improvement skills. I sell marketing systems for contractors but even people whose job doesn't label them as a salesperson are selling at some point, even if it's trying to get a new boy or girlfriend. You have to sell someone on going out with you.

But here's the issue, when it comes to sales and marketing, salespeople are paid to go out and make sales and bring profits into THEIR company, not yours. When really what you're looking for is a marketing program to bring money to you. They'll try to convince you marketing with them is the best place in town and really works because they have 150,000 readers, listeners, watchers of what ever it is their company caters too.

So how do you know who to deal with and who is the person or company that's going to actually make YOU money? Below you'll see 4 mistakes to avoid when hiring a marketing company. Avoiding these and you'll be much further along the path of getting a marketing system to bring you some cold hard cash!

Ready? Let's go...

1. **Choosing a marketing company who does not offer accurately tracked and measured marketing methods.**
   Putting your money into a marketing campaign and not having

any idea what your return on investment is, is really just a huge waste of time, energy and most importantly, money! Luckily, there are many marketing campaigns that do offer a measurable result. Whether it's getting tracked with what I think is one of the greatest tools at your disposal, a tracking phone number. (a tracking phone number will tell you exactly what marketing campaign somebody called you from). Or a landing page on your website. Using either of these tracking tools will give you the ability to figure out how many people responded as a result of your individual marketing methods. Choosing a marketing campaign that is not measurable, in my opinion, is absolutely worthless. You've probably been there and done that, maybe numerous times. Don't worry, we all have, it's actually how I learned these methods about marketing. I spent a lot of money marketing my business and wasn't getting any jobs as a result. I knew there had to be a better way and luckily I found it, now you have it too. When you're done reading this book you'll be able to market your business from an informed and educated position.

And, as an added bonus, if you choose a marketing campaign that is measurable and give's you measurable results you are creating an asset to your company. Knowing and having proof your marketing campaigns work and what kind of profit they generate, gives you total control of your business, you can turn these campaigns up or down depending on your income needs any time you choose. It will also make your company's valuation worth more, give you more money in your pocket, letting you hire more employees and even sleep better at night knowing you finally have 100% control of your business and your finances.

2. **Choosing a marketing company with a great sales pitch.** I'm sure you've been there, a marketing company is knocking on your door and wanting to talk to you about selling you some type of marketing. Those people are typically great sales people and have great sales pitches, but they are terrible marketers. Most of the time, they will offer to create a message or an ad for you. Almost one hundred percent of the time this is the wrong approach. Because they don't really know much about your business and they don't have time to find out, their ads will talk about old world craftsmanship and how you've been in business for twenty years and that kind of thing. Those are the things nobody but you really cares about. I like to call those ego ads. It's the same with the ads you see on television with some 4 year old telling you what kind of roofing to buy! First of all I'm pretty sure a 4 year old doesn't have a clue about roofing. The only reason they're in the ad is the business owners ego. They think their kids are cute and everyone else should too. Maybe they are cute but, this is time to sell and generate a profit not show off your kids. It's purely ego and those ads do not work! (Rant over with) They'll talk about how your company is insured. People do care about those things, but the real think people are looking for and care about most is what is in it for them. What can you do for them? Why should they choose you instead of your competitor who's $20 cheaper? Those are the things your marketing needs to talk about. Typically the salesperson who knocks on your door, wanting to sell you advertising, does not go in that direction. So be careful of salespeople who have a great sales pitch.

3. **Choosing a company who does not understand marketing is about making you money.** You will hear a lot of people talk about getting your brand out there and getting your name out in

front of people. That's okay. Your name does need to be in front of people, but your name should be in front of the right people. If they are big on discussing branding and how a person needs to see your ad eight or ten times before they buy you should be raising the red flag! I heard this story the other day and it demonstrated the difference between branding and direct response advertising very well. If we were in a room of three hundred people and I were to invite you to come up on stage, pass out your business card to everyone and talk to them about your business for three minutes, would you take me up on it? Before you answer, let me give you the second option. The second option is, I have a guy in the back of the room who can come up and give you the names of fifty people sitting in the audience right now who are actively searching for a contractor to complete a project in the next three months and we can give you a list with all 50 names addresses, contact information and household income.

Which one would be more valuable? Would it be better for you to just get up and talk in front of three hundred people and hand out your business card, not knowing if they were renters, homeowners or even if they had any interest at all in a contractor (branding approach) or know exactly who the people are in the room looking your services right now (direct response approach)? If you chose option number two and you'd take the fifty people needing your services right now, you picked the least expensive, most profitable method of marketing your business. This is how your marketing should be targeted as well. How could a program like this make you money? If you send a letter to those fifty people you know are getting ready to do a project in their home, how many could you possibly get appointments with? Probably the majority. That's the result of direct response marketing and success in business is very much dependent on what sort of markcting campaigns you choose. As a side benefit, it's also a lot of fun knowing you have full control of how much money you'll make next week and the week after and the month after that.

4. **Choosing a company who never ask you questions or fully understands your business – and what's more, your client.**
In this case, of course a marketing company is never going to fully understand your business as well as you do. They do need to know and understand what goals you have, where you're company is headed, what kind of person is your best client and what kind of people are you targeting? Are you targeting high end homes? The very affluent people? Are you targeting middle class? Upper middle class? Who is the client you're looking for? What are the goals for your company? Most sales people never ask what client you're looking for or anything about your business, mainly because they are only concerned with selling you ad space on their radio station, TV station or wherever they are calling on you from. They will just blast your message and it's pretty much useless, because the majority of people hearing the ad are not going to be your correct target prospect. So don't choose a marketing company who doesn't care to know anything about your business. Here's how you can spot this in action – you write them a check, you hand them a check and they go make you a commercial. If this is their system, you'll have an ad that talks about old world value or craftsmanship, you've been in business for twenty years, you're insured and "Come on down and see us." And, the ad is going to fall flat! I would highly recommend you stay away from those salespeople and their businesses.

# Why You Want A Trackable No Staff Marketing System

First of all, this kind of system works on autopilot 24/7. It doesn't get sick, it doesn't take lunches, it continues to work for you all day, all night, every day, seven days a week 365 days a year. There is no employee ever going to be able to do that for you.

Next it removes human error. As people we have some flaws and we make errors, I'm sure you've had your share, some are easier to fix than others. Having a system that predictably works every time you set it in motion removes the vast majority of errors. Once you get a system like this is set up, it's done and all you have to do at that point is decide how often you want to run it to get the sales dollars you need for your business this month.

> 50% of marketing works and 50% doesn't. I just wish I knew which 50 it was that worked!"
>
> Jack Welsh, CEO GE

Wouldn't it be nice if when you noticed your bank account was running a little low you had a salesperson you could call and tell them, "Ok, here's the deal. I need $100,000 in sales and I need it by this time next month!" and, you could be certain they'd pull it off for you? Well that's what having a trackable no staff marketing system is like. Except, you don't have to call up a salesperson, all you have to do is set your system in motion and it does the rest. In the very beginning you won't be able to know your exact results will look like but after you've run the system a few times you'll be able to look at the tracking details and know within a reasonable dollar amount what it will produce for you each and every time you run it. At this point doing a little bit of simple math will easily tell you exactly what you need to do to reach that sales level you're striving for.

Next, it's going to save you money by taking advantage of the ability to track your ads which by the way almost no business does. This will save you a ton of money by allowing you to see exactly what ads are working best. No more just cutting out a random bunch of marketing, but only spending money on marketing and processes you know are proven to work. Ho much could you save by cutting out all the waste you're spending right now and not getting return on?

It will give you more time to play golf, take a vacation, just relax and lower your stress level. Knowing how much you can reasonably expect to see in sales in your business next week takes away a huge chunk of stress. A system like this is also going to allow you to make payroll without worrying about where is the money going to come from. I remember when I was contracting, knowing payroll was coming up used to tie my stomach in knots. I knew my employees were depending on me, I had to make it happen.

If you choose to use these methods of marketing to take control of your business and start making more money there are many fringe benefits as well. You can hire a new assistant to do the things in your business you're doing now but hate, like filing, paying bills and answering the phone. You can put those chores on somebody else. Hire an assistant, have them screen your calls and only take the calls to increase your business. Do the things in your business you're really good at. Now you'll be controlling your business rather than your business controlling you.

Control of your business gives you a lot of flexibility and allows you to determine what type of jobs you contract. Have you ever contracted a job you really didn't want but went ahead and signed the contract anyway because you needed the money? I know I did and it was awful. Typically those homeowners were the hardest people to work for and I wasn't even getting the benefit of enjoying what I was doing, I wasn't making the money I knew I should be making on the job and the list went on. If you've been in this situation you know it isn't fun. When you start to implement systems like this in your business, you will start getting the jobs you'd like and being able to pass on the one's you'd rather not deal with. Maybe you enjoy siding jobs, building sun rooms or decks, whatever it is you enjoy most, implementing a focused marketing system will allow you to specialize, and, specialists always make more money that people who choose to "do it all". You'll make more money and you'll be a lot happier all because you're finally in control.

You can also de-commoditize your business with a marketing system like this. With traditional marketing you and your competition all look alike! Why should the prospect choose you?

A trackable, no staff marketing system sets you apart from your competition. It tells your prospects why they should be doing business with you and why you are the clear choice over your competitors. When you have that you'll be able to charge higher prices and still increase your closing ratio for jobs booked. You may not believe me now, but I challenge you to give this a try and see it absolutely 100% does work.

Imagine no longer being just one of 100 siding, deck or roofing companies in town. Now you will be THE siding, deck or roofing company in town to do business with, as a result of marketing, people will know, like and trust you and your company as well as recognize you as the local expert and choose you when they are ready to upgrade their homes.

Marketing like this is also known as selling in advance and during the marketing process sells your customers on doing business with you. Now their first question isn't going to be how much do you charge. It's going to be when can you look at my project and tell me what needs to be done. And, the best part of all... they are willing to pay you more money for it because your marketing system will be doing all the selling up front, before you ever talk to the prospect.

So with that, now you've de-commoditized your business you can raise your prices and make more profit than you ever have in the past. I challenge you, just give it a try and see how it works for your business.

# The Consequence (and difference) Of Value And Price

Price is what you pay. Value is what you get.
When you choose a marketing company, you'll have a wide variety of choices in marketing methods and pricing you will be offered. If you choose your marketing campaign based solely on price, you'll obviously get the cheapest marketing for your company and your returns will likely reflect the cheap choice in that you'll see very small returns and in many cases no returns on your investment what so ever.

Richard Branson, one of the most prolific and out of the box business marketers of our time in my opinion. Often in his earlier days of building his business into the billions of dollars worth of profit he enjoys today, he really understood this concept.

He'd choose marketing methods costing hundreds or even thousands of dollars but he was always looking for methods which would result in much more value to his business than he spent. Value could mean you get a 10x return on your investment or could give you much more. The key here is return on investment (ROI). If you could purchase a marketing piece that was sure to add the value of superior control and sure fire money making methods, what would it be worth to you?
Adding a repeatable marketing system to your business now will not only make you money right now, but it adds to the overall value of your business.

Think about this, how much value would be added to your business if you had a predictable system in place bringing new customers every week like clockwork. Yet you never had to talk to a prospect until they absolutely knew you were the right contractor for them and were ready to sign the contract to get started? A lot right?

# 100% No Risk Guarantee

If you offer a guarantee make sure you prospect knows about it. A rock solid guarantee can cause a prospect to choose you over your competition even when all other deciding factors are the same.

Take a look at our Guarantee, this may give you some ideas:

## Satisfaction Guaranteed

This means operational and working as agreed or it's FREE! Every product we supply to you comes with our no risk guarantee. **If it's a website** it means it's working to your satisfaction. If you're not happy we'll fix the problem area absolutely free.

**Marketing campaign** exact returns on investment will vary from industry to industry and cannot be guaranteed. Although the type of marketing methods we've talked about in this book have been used in numerous industries and made many people extremely wealthy.

If it's a **marketing method or product** you've purchased from us and you feel it isn't worth 12 times what you paid for it, just let us know within 365 days and we'll refund your money ASAP! That's how <u>DARN certain</u> I am that our methods will give <u>you the tools your business needs</u> to bring in new leads and customers to your business *fast!*

## Four Steps To A Profitable Marketing System

**Step 1:** Make the commitment to yourself and your business to spend some time each week doing something to market your business. Your business is either on the move and growing or dying.
You must be marketing to keep your business strong, healthy, growing and making a living for you and your employees. Done right, this will create a far above average living for you and the people who depend on you.

**Step 2:** List your objectives. Creating any sort of marketing campaign without objectives will not work. Are you looking to simply grow a prospects list or do you want to increase sales by 67%? Know what your goals are and track your efforts to make sure they are taking you there.

**Step 3:** Ask questions. If you know your objectives, ask the experts how to best get there. This can take years off of how long it takes you to get the business to the level you want it to be.

**\*\*Note\*\*** As we said in the beginning of this book you're invited to call us. We've dedicated our business to educating contractors and we will be happy to help you achieve results in your business.

**Step 4:** Once you're satisfied you're working with an honest ethical professional, invite them to take a look at your business. Ask them to offer suggestions on how they can help you increase your profits.
A written quote will give you the assurance of knowing exactly how much your job will cost and will make sure you avoid any surprises.

# The "One Second" In House Marketing Analysis

After reading this you'll literally be able to simply think about your existing marketing and determine whether or not the money you've spent on it is money well spent.

To really understand why this works it's important to understand marketing from the prospects view. If you step into the prospects shoes for a minute and think about what it is you'd want in a contractor, what do you come up with?
1. A contractor I can trust.
2. A contractor who will do the best job possible.
3. To know the contractor I choose is not going to rip me off!
4. A contractor who will get the job done so I can get my life in order again.

What did you come up with? Close to what is listed here? So what does this really mean? It means prospects are worried about what you can and will do for them. Most marketing is not geared to answer the nagging question your prospects have in the back of their mind. The one question they very desperately want answered and that is: drum roll please... "What is in it for me!?

If your marketing is not answering that for your prospects I guarantee you are losing prospects that should have turned into cold hard cash paying customers.

Ok, so that's the why, now what you've been waiting for. The how. I told you it would only take you one second to know if your marketing dollars are well spent, so if you want to test me set your stop watch right now before you continue reading... Ok ready set? Does your marketing use the word "we, I or us"? Stop watch off!

The answer is either yes or no. I'm not much of a betting man but I will wager your answer was yes.

If you answered yes, your marketing dollars are not generating the leads your business deserves.

So, now you know your leads and sales can and should be better, how do you change it up and squeeze every last customer out of those dollars you are spending? I'm going to tell you right now.

This is going to be an easy fix for you and just because it's easy I don't want you to minimize how powerful this is going to be for you. This one simple change could potentially add hundreds of thousands of dollars to your business.

Go through your marketing and take every place I, we or us is mentioned and replace it with "you". When you make this easy change you are now talking the customers language (it's all about them) and you will have no choice but to tell them what they get or how your business will help them.

Some of the verbiage in your marketing may not make sense anymore with this change. If you can't reorganize a sentence or phrase to fit "you" instead of "I", "we" or "us", get rid of it, Your prospect really doesn't care.

If you want to take this further and think about how this little change will set you apart from your competition, open up the Yellow Pages to your desired listing, Roofing, Siding, Home Improvement, it doesn't matter. What do you see? Just in case you don't have your copy of the Yellow pages handy, I'll save you some time and tell you a few of the things listed in my Yellow Pages.

1. Quality work at a fair price
2. Tear offs (I know what this is but does the average prospect? I bet they just expect it, if you want to know how to capitalize on this, take me up on my free offer at the end of this book)
3. Call us for best price and installation
4. Member of BBB since 1985  (Yawn... Who cares?)
5. Tear off, Ree-Roof, Quality work. (Ree-Roof is not a typo here it is actually printed that way)
6. We keep the drips from dripping in!
7. Repair specialists
8. Roofing specialists
9. 30 years experience

The list goes on and on, standard run of the mill ads not setting any one company apart from their competition. When everyone looks the same the only way customers have to choose is by price. Be sure your business is different.

Obviously, I looked up roofing and as you can see these are all "I", "we" and "us"statements that really don't tell your prospect anything.The prospects looking at those ads probably expect you can re-roof, install or stop a leaky roof just by the fact your business is listed under roofing. All of these ads are completely useless because they don't tell the prospect anything but what the company does - which is roofing.

Now imagine your ad is among all of those "me too" ads but, your ad says something like "Discover How To Get The Best Roof Installed On Your House For The Best Price". From there the ad would direct the prospect to a website where they'd read your report on exactly how to get the best roof for the best possible price. Notice I didn't say the cheapest price, the best is never the cheapest. Also they would have your contact info in the report. If you'd rather have them call for the report you could also mail it out, however people will be afraid they're going to talk to a sales person and for that reason I'd stick to the downloadable report or a free recorded message.

In your report you've told them all the ins and outs as well as the pitfalls to watch out for, who do you think they're going to call to check out their roof and give a proposal? That's right, YOU!

You've now set yourself apart from your competition by giving the prospect something with value. This gives them the opportunity to know, like and trust you. You are now miles ahead of your competitors when it comes to the likelihood of getting the job. This is the same with every other category of construction as well.

If you doubt me just do me a favor and test it out. Do a small mailing offering a report like this. It'll work, I promise! Oh yeah, this one may really get your head shaking but DO NOT put your logo on the ad. Just the simple statement we talked about above and where they can go to get the report.

You will need to have a way to track the visits to the webpage to see the true results. Google analytics is a simple and free program which will allow you to do that.

I'd love to hear your results when you do this. Please email at david@affluentcontractor.com or call me at 423-443-4254 and let me know how this works for you.

# The Home Improvement Contractors Guide To Marketing & Sales

As I said before this simple little change could bring in hundreds of thousands of dollars! If you implement a trackable no staff marketing system like we've discussed throughout this book it'll not only be worth thousands or hundreds of thousands of dollars to you and your business, but it'll truly put you in control of your business.

Giving you the time to play with family and friends and know you're going to have prospects calling you next week, because you have a system in place working for you.

There are two ways to grow your business, one is work harder and more hours so you can get more done and who wants to do that? I sure don't and I doubt you do either. The other way is to put systems in place that will leverage the work you currently do which is exactly what creating your own trackable no staff selling system will do for you.

# Wrap Up

You're now fully equipped to go out and interview marketing companies. You'll easily and quickly determine if they are up to the challenge of bringing you back more money than you spend with them.

We do suggest you implement a whole no staff marketing system if you'd like to save yourself time, make more money and have less frustration. Even with full implementation you don't have to go wild and spend big money right out of the gate.

If you're on the fence and thinking maybe this is a bunch of hype, do a small test and prove to yourself it works.

If you'd like to take the hassle out of your business and gain total control with a Trackable No Staff Marketing System for your business we'd be happy to help you get started. And, because you've read this book you can get started for free and without obligation.

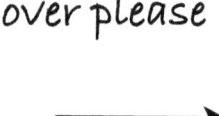

over please

# The Home Improvement Contractors Guide To Marketing & Sales

## "Special FREE Bonus Offer Worth $497.00"

Because you've read this book and proven you are the kind of take action business person who wants to improve your business, we want to make you this special offer to help you get started fast and making more money fast!

Take action for you and your business. Begin attracting your ideal customers to your business with this time tested, easy to implement SYSTEM that works regardless of what the economy is doing!

Simply cash in your Special FREE Bonus Offer by visiting the webpage listed below for a **100% free of charge marketing analysis** of your business.

1. With this analysis you'll discover the holes where your marketing dollars are slipping away to never return.
2. How to plug those holes and get a road map of steps to implement to build your own Trackable No Staff Marketing System. (The easy way)
3. The single most lucrative marketing method which *costs almost nothing* yet crushes any other form of marketing you can do, even if you pay thousands!

## Visit www.affluentcontractor.com/freebonus

To our success,

*David Hawke*

David Hawke

www.ingramcontent.com/pod-product-compliance
Lightning Source LLC
Chambersburg PA
CBHW071643170526
45166CB00003B/1405